# Pumpkin Finds His Feelings

Written & Illustrated by
## Andrea Realpe

Angy's Books

Angy's Books

Copyright © 2021 Andrea Realpe

All rights reserved. No part of this book may be reproduced or transmitted in any form or by any means, electronic, or mechanical, including photocopying, recording, or by any information storage and retrieval system, without the prior written permission from the author.
Visit us online for more information: Angysbooks.com

ISBN: 9780578306131

The art for this book was created with graphite pencils, watercolors, digital ink and loads of love.

# THIS BOOK BELONGS TO ...

_____

Dedicated to:

Everyone in search of their feelings.

For my inspiration and my word, Mathias and my sweet husband, Mat for all the support and love.

On a cold breezy day on Parklane, Cody carved a pumpkin. He gave him eyes, a nose, and a smile.

When Cody was done, he placed Pumpkin on the top of the steps of his purple porch and lit his candle.

Cody loved his pumpkin and Pumpkin loved him back.

Once Cody had gone inside, Pumpkin happily looked around with a smile. He watched the moon and the stars shining brightly in the sky.

Suddenly, a WHOOSH of icy wind blew out the light inside him. Now, despite his stuck-on smile, Pumpkin couldn't feel anything at all.

The happy, the sad, the angry, and the fearful. His shell became brisk, empty, and cold.
No glimmer or glow. He had to do something, to turn his light back on. So he began to search.

In search for his feelings, Pumpkin walked and walked and walked until he saw a farm.
On this farm, he saw a scarecrow.

"Are you okay?" whispered Pumpkin.
Scarecrow whimpered, "I'm scared."
"It's okay to feel scared," said Pumpkin.

"Even if I'm supposed to scare and not be scared?" asked Scarecrow. "Yes, even then," said Pumpkin. "Look at me. I always look happy, but I don't feel anything at all."

Pumpkin then asked Scarecrow, "have you seen my feelings?" "What kind of feelings?" said Scarecrow. "The feelings that make your tummy feel warm and joyful or the feelings that make your eyes tear up?"

The happy, the sad, the angry or the scared or any feeling besides no feeling at all, that would be better," replied Pumpkin.
"I haven't seen your feelings. Let's ask Cat."

Pumpkin walked and walked and walked until he came across a maple tree with red-orange leaves. On this tree was a cat.

The cat was happily playing with the falling autumn leaves.

"You look so happy. Do you know where I can find happiness?" Pumpkin asked.
"Maybe if you try something new and different. Catching leaves makes me happy. Do you want to try?" Cat asked.

With the leaves swirling all-around, Pumpkin and Cat jumped and leaped. But Pumpkin didn't feel anything at all.

"This isn't working. I can't seem to find my feelings," said Pumpkin.
"What kind of feelings?" replied Cat.
"Any Feelings. I always look happy, but I feel nothing at all," said Pumpkin.
"I haven't seen your feelings, Pumpkin. Maybe Turkey knows where they are."

Pumpkin walked and walked and walked until he saw a field. On this field, he saw a turkey.

Turkey puffed up his chest and flapped his wings and angrily charged at Pumpkin. But Pumpkin didn't feel scared, he didn't feel anything at all.

"What are you doing here? I'm busy. I haven't found food in days and I'm angry," shouted Turkey.
"I have an idea. You can eat a piece of my stem. I don't need it," said Pumpkin. This made Turkey feel better and less angry.

"Can you help me feel angry like you?" asked Pumpkin. "Maybe," said Turkey. "Try crossing your arms and scrunching up your face until it's red and think about things that make you mad."

Pumpkin crossed his arms and scrunched his face and tried thinking angry thoughts, but he didn't feel angry. He didn't feel anything at all.
"It's not working," Pumpkin said. "Hmm. Maybe Cody knows how to find your feelings," said Turkey.

Pumpkin walked and walked and walked until he saw a house with a purple porch. On this porch, he saw Cody sitting on the stairs. Cody was sad. He had lost his favorite pumpkin.

Pumpkin stood behind a tree and watched as Cody wiped tears from his cheeks. He didn't like seeing his friend cry. Seeing Cody so sad began to make Pumpkin sad too.

But the sadness didn't last long. Pumpkin quickly realized that if he was feeling sad then he must be feeling.

It was better to feel happy, scared, angry, or sad than not feel anything at all. This made Pumpkin smile with joy and run to Cody.

When Cody saw Pumpkin he gave him a big hug and said, "I found you!"
Pumpkin, with a smile and a glowing light inside, hugged him back and said, "and I found my feelings."

Made in United States
North Haven, CT
05 October 2024

58379099R00018